My AMAZING Book of

Programs

by Kiki Prottsman
Illustrated by Maha Younus

vol. 1
JavaScript

About the author:

Kiki Prottsman is an award-winning educational designer with a master's degree in computer science and more than 200 full-service elementary school lessons beneath her belt.

As the former Executive Director of Thinkersmith, Kiki made her name creating offline activities that introduce students to the concepts behind programming. After joining Code.org in 2013, Kiki began to develop online lessons for young programmers as well.

Having provided oversight to dozens of exercises included in the annual Hour of Code™ event, it is estimated that Kiki's activities have reached more than 200 million learners across the globe. If you are ready to try programming for the first time, you really should use a guide with her name on it.

Written by **Kiki Prottsman**
Edited by **Nicole Reitz-Larsen**
Illustrated by **Maha Younus**

Special thanks to
James & Jackson Davis
Terri, Parker, & Keagan Savage

and major supporters
Heather King, Bryan Adams,
and
Michael Barrow in support of Girl Power!

First Edition, 2020
Copyright ©2020 Kiki Prottsman

www.KiKIvsIT.com

Contents

Dear Parents,

Congratulations for making the choice to introduce your kiddos to a subject that's creative, fun, and useful!

Programming can be very difficult, but this book has been thoughtfully written to introduce a specific language and important concepts in a way that is simple and easy to follow. If at any time your child gets stuck, please encourage them to explain what they know and have them try to describe the problem that they are having. This is the first step in helping your child to debug problems on their own!

In the event that your child gets to a place where their struggle is no longer productive, I have provided QR codes to scan for helpful resources.

Though tempting, please try your hardest not to swoop in and take over the mouse, keyboard, or navigation for your child. Frustration plays a crucial role in learning and this book expertly balances opportunities for frustration with opportunities for success. Neither is as meaningful without the other.

Happy coding!

Getting started
(Your new playground)

There are lots of ways to write JavaScript.
In this book, we recommend **https://repl.it**.
It allows you to create an account (with your
parent's permission) so you can save and
share your code online!

This is where your code will run!

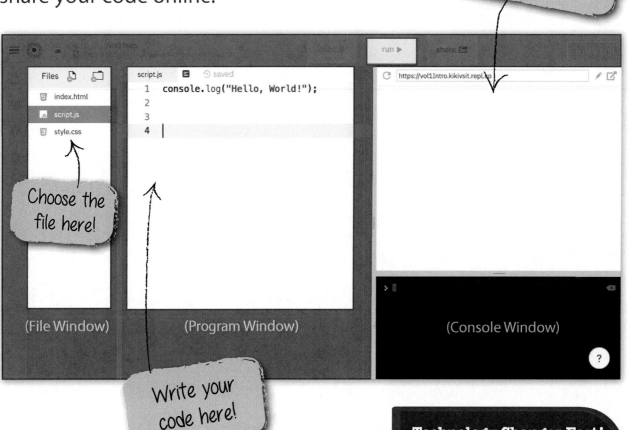

Choose the file here!

(File Window)   (Program Window)   (Console Window)

Write your code here!

In the rest of this book, we'll play
with programs that have already
been started. Click on the correct
file in the file window, then edit
the code in the program window.

Technology Changes Fast!

Nothing lasts forever and
websites are no exception!

If the recommended site
doesn't work anymore, visit
bit.ly/editJSonline
for other options!

Now is a great time to figure out what the icons and buttons in your programming environment do. Can you figure out how you will run your code? Is there a way to share it? Download it? Are there any other settings to play with?

Scan this with a QR Code reader to watch Kiki explain repl.it

Your turn!

When you play with programs, you should know that you are in complete control of the computer! You don't always have to write exactly what this book tells you!

Sometimes when you change something the program will stop working. No need to worry. Just put it back and try changing something else instead. Pretty soon, you'll figure out what everything does. It's a great way to learn on your own.

Make sure you keep track of the edits you make along the way (in case you want to undo something.)

Hello, World!
(My first program)

Scan to watch Kiki program "Hello, world!"

It's a tradition with coders to test out a new programming language by getting the computer to say "Hello, World!" It's not the most exciting sentence, but you can change it to something else later if you want to.

Capitalization matters! Make sure to pay attention to the letter case.

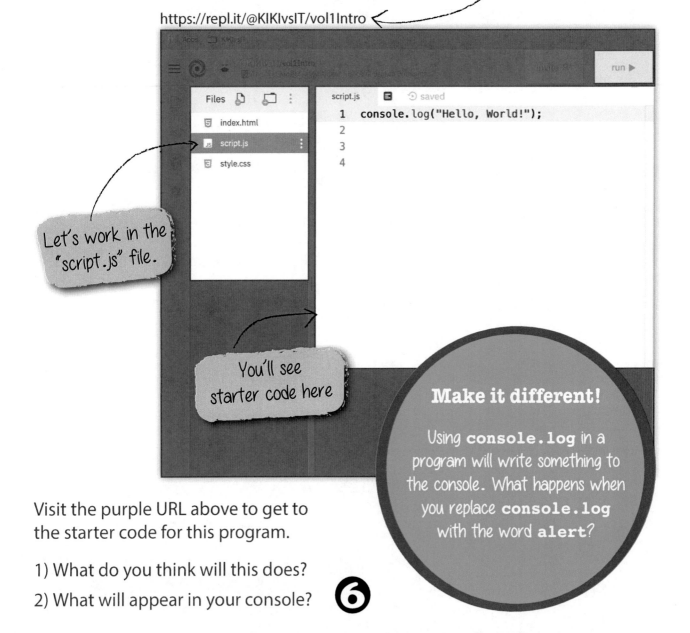

https://repl.it/@KIKIvsIT/vol1Intro

Let's work in the "script.js" file.

You'll see starter code here

Make it different!

Using **console.log** in a program will write something to the console. What happens when you replace **console.log** with the word **alert**?

Visit the purple URL above to get to the starter code for this program.

1) What do you think will this does?

2) What will appear in your console?

❻

What can you change in this program? Try the "banana" test! Replace words from the program with the word banana (one at a time) and see which changes keep your program running, and which make your program break. Make sure to change the program back between tries!

Scan this to see some fun changes that you can make to the "Hello, World!" program

Can you guess what will work and what won't?

Let's break it down...

console.log

This writes a message to the console.

( )

The parentheses hold the message that belongs to **console.log**.

" "

The quotes surround a string of text to tell the computer that it should use your words exactly as you entered them.

;

The semicolon tells the computer that you are finished with that line of instruction.

What did you try?

Click me
(Connecting JavaScript to HTML)

Scan to learn more
about how to use JS with HTML

In this book, we'll divide our code into three parts:

1) **The HTML file** - This will contain the code that tells the webpage what to load when you click "run".

2) **The JavaScript file** - This is where we'll spend most of our time.

3) **The CSS file** - This is where the style rules are written.

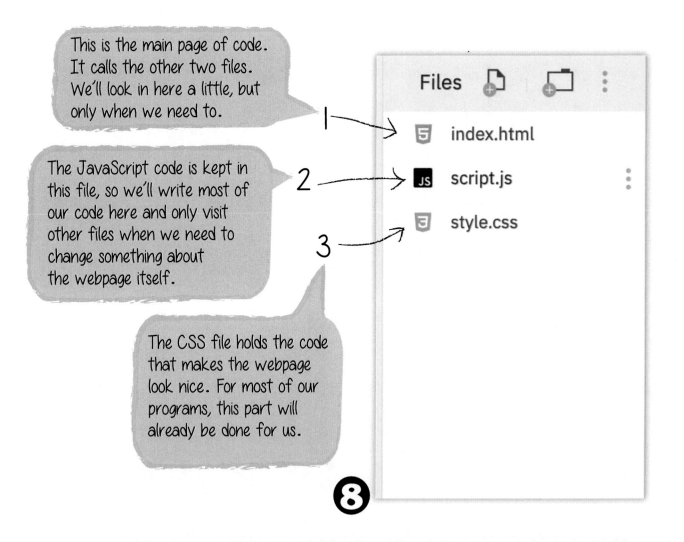

This is the main page of code. It calls the other two files. We'll look in here a little, but only when we need to.

The JavaScript code is kept in this file, so we'll write most of our code here and only visit other files when we need to change something about the webpage itself.

The CSS file holds the code that makes the webpage look nice. For most of our programs, this part will already be done for us.

Files

index.html

script.js

style.css

❽

Visit **https://repl.it/@KIKIvsIT/clickMe** to see the code for the next program. When you click run, it should work. But what will it do?

https://repl.it/@KIKIvsIT/clickMe

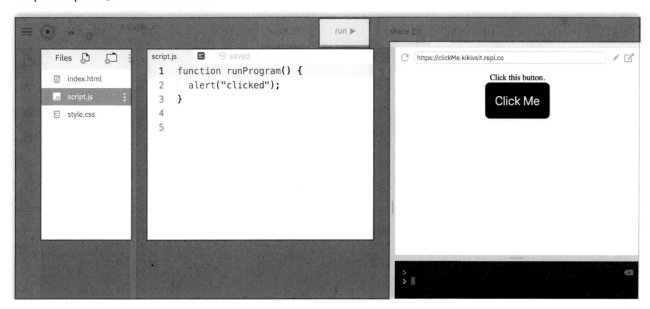

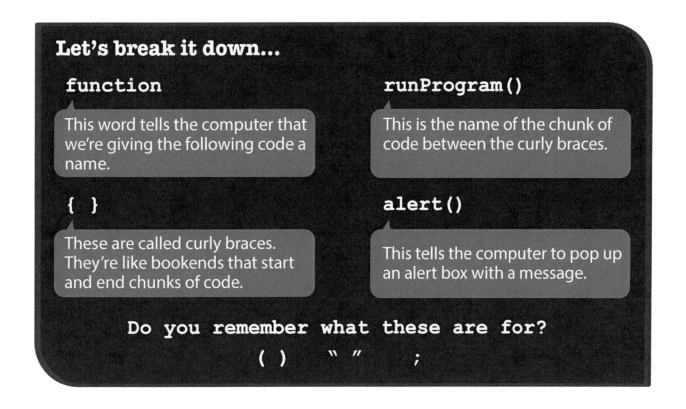

Let's break it down...

function

This word tells the computer that we're giving the following code a name.

runProgram()

This is the name of the chunk of code between the curly braces.

{ }

These are called curly braces. They're like bookends that start and end chunks of code.

alert()

This tells the computer to pop up an alert box with a message.

Do you remember what these are for?

( )   " "   ;

It doesn't work!
(Finding bugs in the code)

Watch Kiki go through
the debugging process

This program is broken. It has a **bug** (which means it has an error.)
Can you compare it to the other programs and figure out why it's
not working? What happens when you click the blue button?

https://repl.it/@KIKIvsIT/oopsie

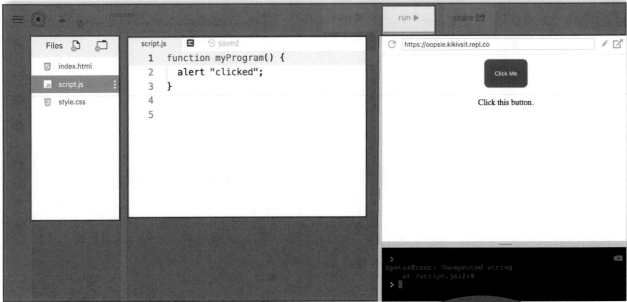

Remember that you need to click

before the website will load, then
you need to click

before the function will run.

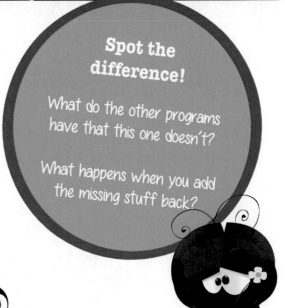

Spot the difference!

What do the other programs
have that this one doesn't?

What happens when you add
the missing stuff back?

The console will give you a hint about what the error is and where the bug can be found.

Reading the console

SyntaxError: Unexpected string

> This lets us know that something is written in the wrong way, and that thing is a **string** that the computer doesn't expect to see yet.

at /script.js:2:9

> This tells us that the place where the computer gets confused is in the file "script.js" on line 2, at position 9. (That's where it expects to see something else.)

ReferenceError: myProgram is not defined
at HTMLButtonElement.onclick (/:12:37)

> Because there's an error inside the myProgram function, the file doesn't recognize the definition! Fix the bug and this will go away, too.

What did you try?	What happened?

You might notice that it's not just one thing that's missing, it's a set of things! Did you figure that out? Did the console help?

Sometimes you get an idea, but lose it before you can get to the computer to try it.

It can be helpful to have paper handy when you're working through problems.

(Also, you can take notes here.)

12

Who are you?
(Getting input)

Get a run-through of the code

Getting input from a user is really easy with JavaScript. We just need to use the prompt command. Clicking the button in this program will pop up an input box that asks the user's name.

https://repl.it/@KIKIvsIT/whoDis

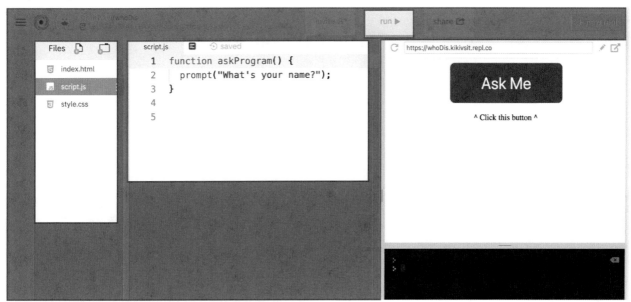

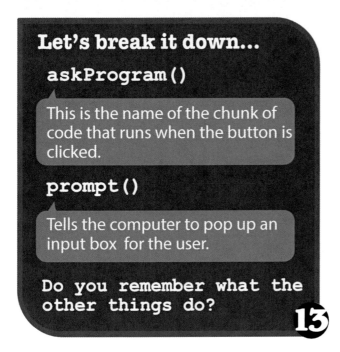

Let's break it down...

askProgram()

This is the name of the chunk of code that runs when the button is clicked.

prompt()

Tells the computer to pop up an input box for the user.

Do you remember what the other things do?

13

Here's what a prompt box looks like in repl.it.

Add your name and click OK then the box will disappear.

You are who?
(Saving input in variables)

Learn more about why we use a variable here

To benefit from the input in the prompt box, we either need to use it right away or we need to save it to a **variable** to use later.

https://repl.it/@KIKIvsIT/uWho

Let's break it down...

```
function theProgram() {
```
This line tells the computer that we've named our function theProgram() and we're about to start defining it.

```
var userName = prompt("What's your name?");
```
This creates a storage container called userName where we put the value entered by the user when we ask their name.

```
alert("Hi " + userName);
```
This pops up an alert box that says "Hi" and repeats the user's name.

```
}
```
Lets the computer know that the definition is done.

14

Variables are **SUPER** helpful! They're like little jars that can hold whatever information you need...even when you don't know what that is.

You might not know what name a user will enter, but you need to be able to use that name later in your program. Variables (like userName) let you hold a place in your code for those values once you get them.

```
function theProgram()  {
                banana
    var userName = prompt("What's your name?");
                      banana
    alert("Hi " + userName);
}
```

Cha...cha...cha...changes!

What if we wanted to know someone's favorite animal instead of their name?

What would you change the variable name to?
How else would you change the program?

Make some edits and run your new program to see if it makes sense. You might have to play with it more than once (maybe more than five times) to get it to work the way you want.

Variable soup

(There's a bug in my variable!)

When you're done, scan this to watch Kiki debug this program

Variables make programs interesting, but they also introduce a lot of places for bugs to hide.

Your variable needs to be spelled exactly the same way everywhere you use it. It can't have any spaces and it can't start with a number. Also, capitalization matters!

https://repl.it/@KIKIvsIT/bugSoup

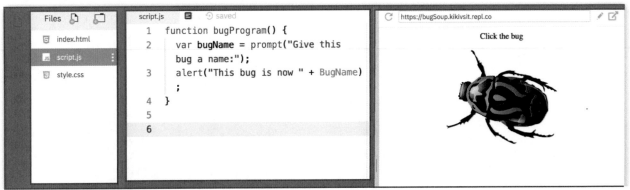

```
script.js                 saved
1   function bugProgram() {
2     var bugName = prompt("Give this
      bug a name:");
3     alert("This bug is now " + BugName)
      ;
4   }
5
6
```

Click the bug

This program doesn't work right.
Can you figure out what it should do?

This program should:

_____

_____

_____

_____

_____

16

Look at the code carefully to figure out what's wrong.
It's like a mystery that you need to hunt for clues to solve.

```
1  function bugProgram() {
2      var bugName = prompt("Give this
       bug a name:");
3      alert("This bug is now " + BugName)
       ;
4  }
5
6
```

Click the bug

```
ReferenceError: bugName is not defined
    at bugProgram (/script.js:3:29)
    at HTMLButtonElement.onclick (/:15:38)
```

This might LOOK like two lines but it's really just one line that got too long so it wrapped itself down below. The computer still thinks of it all as line 2.

What is the console trying to tell you?

Use this as scratch paper to keep track of ideas.

Making the connection
(How HTML and JavaScript connect)

Let Kiki show you how the files work together

So far, our programs have all started when we click something. It is possible to make other interesting things happen but sometimes we'll need to change stuff in both the JavaScript file and the HTML file.

This next program will show you how the two files connect.

https://repl.it/@KIKIvsIT/theCurtain

Here, we're looking at the HTML file

The HTML files that we'll be playing with have two main parts:

HEAD

- Things to *know*
- Defines the name of the page
- Connects the CSS file (style)
- Connects the JS file (JavaScript)

BODY

- Things to *see*
- Contains text and images
- Connects user actions and events to code in the JS file

Let's take a closer look:

HEAD

`<head>` ←— These groups of words inside angled brackets are called "tags". HTML uses them to section off the code.

🚫 `<meta charset="utf-8">`
`<meta name="viewport" content="width=device-width">`
↳ These details are helpful to the computer, but not to us in this book. You don't need to mess with these.

✓ `<title>Click Me</title>`
↳ Between the <title> tags is the title of the webpage. You can change what's in here, if you want.

🚫 `<link href="style.css" rel="stylesheet" type="text/css" />`
↳ This is the name of the file where the computer looks for the code to make the page look a certain way.

It's all in your <head>

Everything that's supposed to be in the <head> section is already there. You shouldn't need to add or edit anything up there (but you can if you want!)

🚫 `<script src="script.js"></script>`
↳ This is how the page tells the computer where to find the JS code.

`</head>`
↳ This tag closes the head section

BODY

`<body>` ←— This tag starts the section of the code that creates the page that users can see.

🚫 `<div id="theDoc">`
↳ This is the name of the main container that holds the page.

✓ Click the cat ←— Text you can edit!

✓ `<br/><br/>` ←— The tag <br/> adds a blank line (like pressing return.)

✓ `<button onclick="catProgram()"> </button>`
↳ This is what calls the JS function when we click the button.

🚫 `</div>` ←— Ends the main page container

`</body>` ←— Ends the body of the document

Every <body> is different

Most of what changes in the HTML from program to program will be here in the body. If you want to see what makes a page different, check between the <body> and </body> tags.

KEY

✓ Okay to mess with   🚫 Advanced users only

Some <body> to play with:

Let's play around with the code inside the <body> section of this page. A few small changes can make the page your own.

Let's break it down...

```
Click the Cat
```

This line shows up on the webpage exactly how you write it. Go ahead and change it to something else. Does it matter what you change it to?

```
<br/><br/>
```

Each <br/> tag adds another blank line below the words you wrote. Try adding more <br/> tags, or taking one away and see how the page changes.

```
<button onclick="catProgram()"> </button>
```

There's a lot going on with this line! Let's try looking at each piece.

<button> </button>
This is a button tag set. The look of the button is controlled by the style.css file, but the button action is controlled by the onclick line.

onclick=
This part tells the button what to do when it's clicked.

"catProgram()"
This chunk calls our catProgram() function inside the script.js file. Do you think the program will work if you change that piece?

Here's one more thing to try. What happens when you use a different word between the button tags? Try changing it to:
<button onclick="catProgram()"> CAT </button>

Putting it all together

Now that you understand what's happening in the HTML, let's look at the JavaScript for this page to see how it all connects.

https://repl.it/@KIKIvsIT/theCurtain

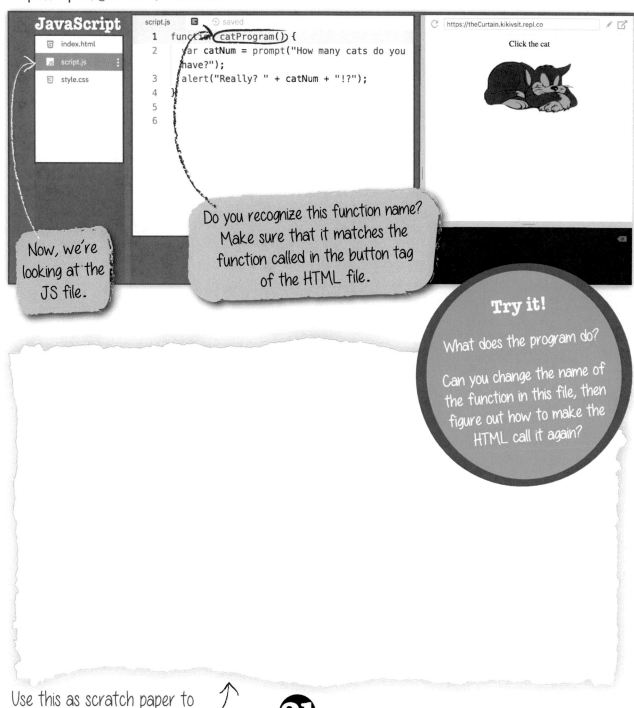

JavaScript

```
script.js                saved
1  function catProgram() {
2      var catNum = prompt("How many cats do you
       have?");
3      alert("Really? " + catNum + "!?");
4  }
5
6
```

https://theCurtain.kikivsit.repl.co

Click the cat

Now, we're looking at the JS file.

Do you recognize this function name? Make sure that it matches the function called in the button tag of the HTML file.

Try it!

What does the program do?

Can you change the name of the function in this file, then figure out how to make the HTML call it again?

Use this as scratch paper to keep track of ideas.

Who's got the button?
(Connect the button to the JavaScript)

Watch Kiki debug
this webpage

One last step before we start getting fancy.

This program doesn't work! Can you look at the JavaScript and the HTML to see if you can figure out how to fix it?

https://repl.it/@KIKIvsIT/bzzt

Go rogue!

Once you fix this, go ahead and make some other changes.

Mess around with anything you want, you won't break the original program!

Click it
(Using images instead of buttons)

For the next set of programs, we're still going to be clicking on pictures but instead of <button> we'll use the <img> tag. This will make it a little easier to get creative.

https://repl.it/@KIKIvsIT/clickit

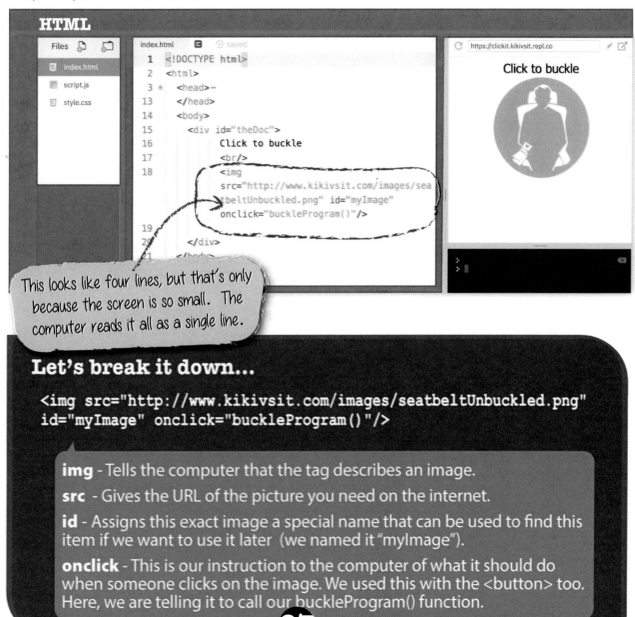

This looks like four lines, but that's only because the screen is so small. The computer reads it all as a single line.

Let's break it down...

```
<img src="http://www.kikivsit.com/images/seatbeltUnbuckled.png"
id="myImage" onclick="buckleProgram()"/>
```

img - Tells the computer that the tag describes an image.

src - Gives the URL of the picture you need on the internet.

id - Assigns this exact image a special name that can be used to find this item if we want to use it later (we named it "myImage").

onclick - This is our instruction to the computer of what it should do when someone clicks on the image. We used this with the <button> too. Here, we are telling it to call our buckleProgram() function.

23

This JavaScript file is a lot like our last few, because it only contains a single function.

If you look closely, though, you'll notice that there's something new and unfamiliar inside.

https://repl.it/@KIKIvsIT/clickit

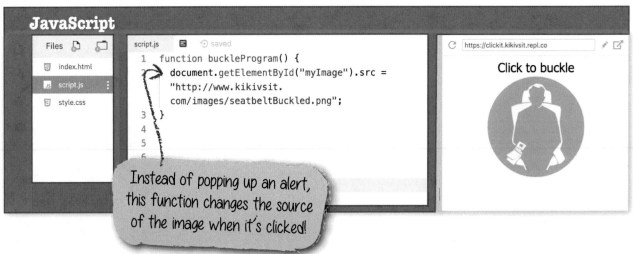

Instead of popping up an alert, this function changes the source of the image when it's clicked!

Let's break it down...

```
document.getElementById("myImage").src =
"http://www.kikivsit.com/images/seatbeltBuckled.png";
```

document
This part tells the computer that we're about to do something to the document that called this function (the HTML page).

getElementById("myImage")
We want to change the element that we named "myImage".

src
We're changing the source URL for the image.

"http://www.kikivsit.com/images/seatbeltBuckled.png";
This is the new URL for the picture that we're changing to.

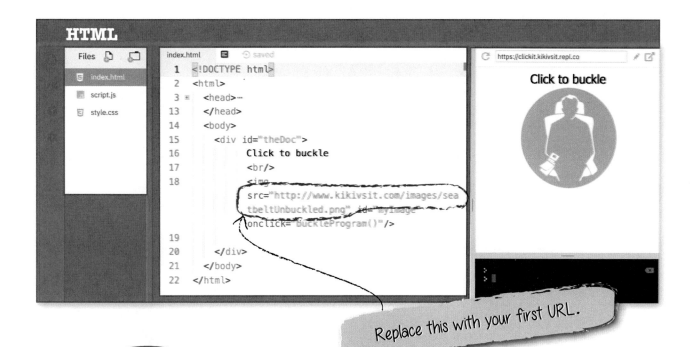

HTML

```
index.html          saved
 1  <!DOCTYPE html>
 2  <html>
 3    <head>…
13    </head>
14    <body>
15      <div id="theDoc">
16          Click to buckle
17          <br/>
18          <img
          src="http://www.kikivsit.com/images/sea
          tbeltUnbuckled.png" id="myImage"
          onclick="BuckleProgram()"/>
19
20      </div>
21    </body>
22  </html>
```

https://clickit.kikivsit.repl.co

Click to buckle

Replace this with your first URL.

Do your own thing

Find a couple of pictures on the internet that you like and copy the URLs to customize this webpage for yourself!

Remember to stick to royalty-free and unlicensed images when looking for content for webpages.

Replace this with your second URL.

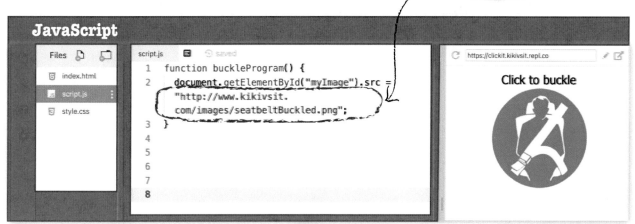

JavaScript

```
script.js          saved
 1  function buckleProgram() {
 2      document.getElementById("myImage").src =
      "http://www.kikivsit.
      com/images/seatbeltBuckled.png";
 3  }
 4
 5
 6
 7
 8
```

https://clickit.kikivsit.repl.co

Click to buckle

Follow the ball

(Where does it all go wrong?)

Watch Kiki play
with this new page

This page builds on what you just learned but takes it to the extreme!
Too bad it doesn't work. Can you play with the webpage and look
at the files to see if you can figure out where it goes wrong?

https://repl.it/@KIKIvsIT/ball

Where's the mistake?

You'll need to play with the page a
little to figure out what's actually
wrong and what's just new.

Bring it all in
(We don't need all those functions!)

What if I told you that we don't need all three functions to make this program work? Let's take advantage of something called a **parameter** to fit all three cups into one function!

https://repl.it/@KIKIvsIT/ball-1

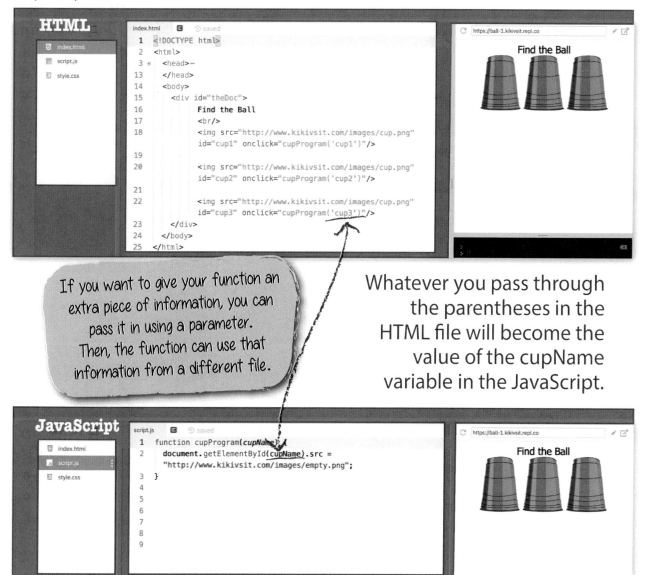

> If you want to give your function an extra piece of information, you can pass it in using a parameter. Then, the function can use that information from a different file.

Whatever you pass through the parentheses in the HTML file will become the value of the cupName variable in the JavaScript.

```html
1  <!DOCTYPE html>
2  <html>
3    <head>--
13   </head>
14   <body>
15     <div id="theDoc">
16         Find the Ball
17         <br/>
18         <img src="http://www.kikivsit.com/images/cup.png"
           id="cup1" onclick="cupProgram('cup1')"/>
19
20         <img src="http://www.kikivsit.com/images/cup.png"
           id="cup2" onclick="cupProgram('cup2')"/>
21
22         <img src="http://www.kikivsit.com/images/cup.png"
           id="cup3" onclick="cupProgram('cup3')"/>
23     </div>
24   </body>
25  </html>
```

```javascript
1  function cupProgram(cupName) {
2    document.getElementById(cupName).src =
     "http://www.kikivsit.com/images/empty.png";
3  }
```

Accounting for differences
(Using conditionals)

Did you notice that the ball went away when we combined the three functions into one? That's because the function didn't treat any of the images differently from the others. We should fix that.

Without changing anything in the HTML file, we can modify our JavaScript to look at the parameter and see if it says "cup3". If so, we'll set the image to the ball. Otherwise (else) we'll set the image to empty. It's that simple!

https://repl.it/@KIKIvsIT/ball-2

```
function cupProgram(cupName) {
    if(cupName == "cup3"){
        document.getElementById(cupName).src =
        "http://www.kikivsit.com/images/ball.png";
    }
    else {
        document.getElementById(cupName).src =
        "http://www.kikivsit.com/images/empty.png";
    }
}
```

Find the Ball

If the value of cupName is set to "cup3", then we'll change the image to a ball.

Or else, we'll set the image to be empty.

Think about it...

Why do we only need 2 options when there are 3 cups?

Can you explain it in your own words?

28

Let's have some fun!
(Make it unpredictable)

More about randomness

That program was fun the first time, but once you know where the ball is going to be, it's just not fun anymore. To keep it spicy, let's add a random element. By randomly choosing what cup will have the ball, we can play this over and over again.

https://repl.it/@KIKIvsIT/ball-3

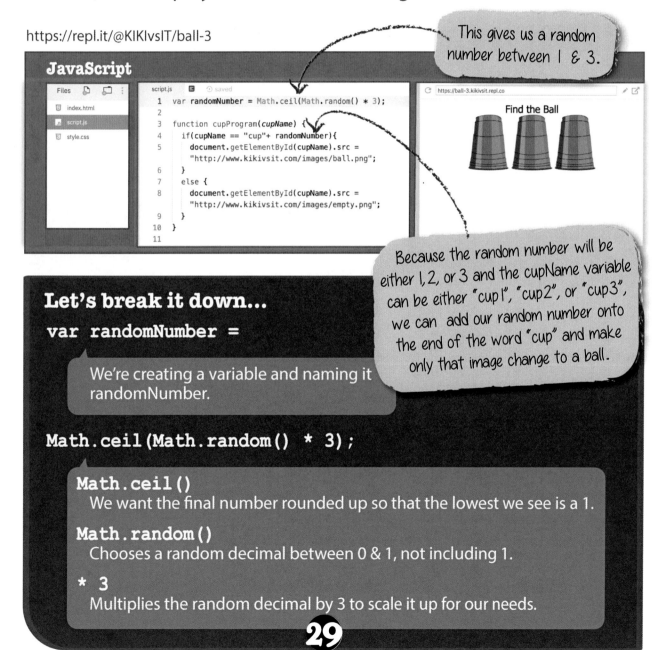

JavaScript

> This gives us a random number between 1 & 3.

```javascript
1   var randomNumber = Math.ceil(Math.random() * 3);
2
3   function cupProgram(cupName) {
4     if(cupName == "cup"+ randomNumber){
5       document.getElementById(cupName).src =
          "http://www.kikivsit.com/images/ball.png";
6     }
7     else {
8       document.getElementById(cupName).src =
          "http://www.kikivsit.com/images/empty.png";
9     }
10  }
11
```

Find the Ball

> Because the random number will be either 1, 2, or 3 and the cupName variable can be either "cup1", "cup2", or "cup3", we can add our random number onto the end of the word "cup" and make only that image change to a ball.

Let's break it down...

var randomNumber =

We're creating a variable and naming it randomNumber.

Math.ceil(Math.random() * 3);

Math.ceil()
We want the final number rounded up so that the lowest we see is a 1.

Math.random()
Chooses a random decimal between 0 & 1, not including 1.

* 3
Multiplies the random decimal by 3 to scale it up for our needs.

29

Collect the coins
(Avoid the gum)

Watch Kiki
debug this

This program is a fun game that uses the skills we've just learned. The only problem is that it doesn't work! Can you figure out why?

https://repl.it/@KIKIvsIT/noGum

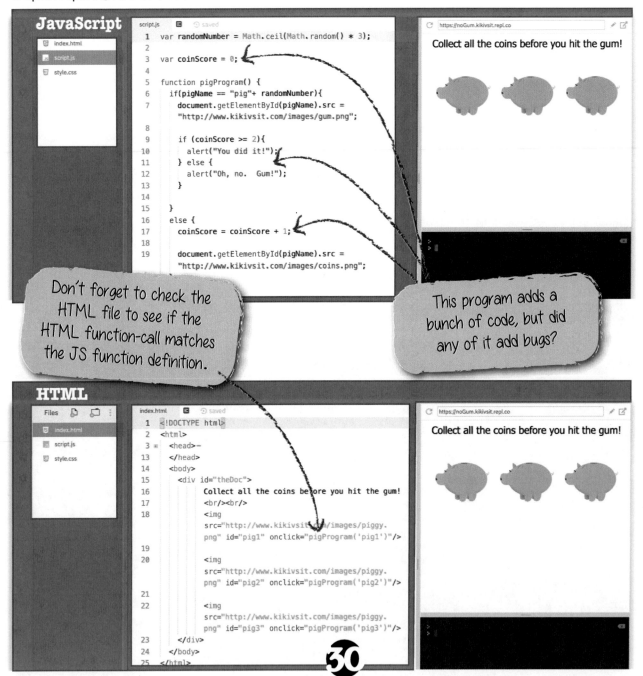

JavaScript

```javascript
var randomNumber = Math.ceil(Math.random() * 3);

var coinScore = 0;

function pigProgram() {
  if(pigName == "pig"+ randomNumber){
    document.getElementById(pigName).src =
    "http://www.kikivsit.com/images/gum.png";

    if (coinScore >= 2){
      alert("You did it!");
    } else {
      alert("Oh, no.  Gum!");
    }

  }
  else {
    coinScore = coinScore + 1;

    document.getElementById(pigName).src =
    "http://www.kikivsit.com/images/coins.png";
```

Collect all the coins before you hit the gum!

Don't forget to check the HTML file to see if the HTML function-call matches the JS function definition.

This program adds a bunch of code, but did any of it add bugs?

HTML

```html
<!DOCTYPE html>
<html>
  <head>-
  </head>
  <body>
    <div id="theDoc">
      Collect all the coins before you hit the gum!
      <br/><br/>
      <img
      src="http://www.kikivsit.com/images/piggy.
      png" id="pig1" onclick="pigProgram('pig1')"/>

      <img
      src="http://www.kikivsit.com/images/piggy.
      png" id="pig2" onclick="pigProgram('pig2')"/>

      <img
      src="http://www.kikivsit.com/images/piggy.
      png" id="pig3" onclick="pigProgram('pig3')"/>
    </div>
  </body>
</html>
```

Collect all the coins before you hit the gum!

30

May I comment?
(Leaving notes in your code)

This program adds even more pigs and also a score tracker! With all of that code, reading the program starts to get confusing, so we've added some secret notes that the computer can't read but we can! Those notes are called comments and they won't change the way your program works.

https://repl.it/@KIKIvsIT/whack

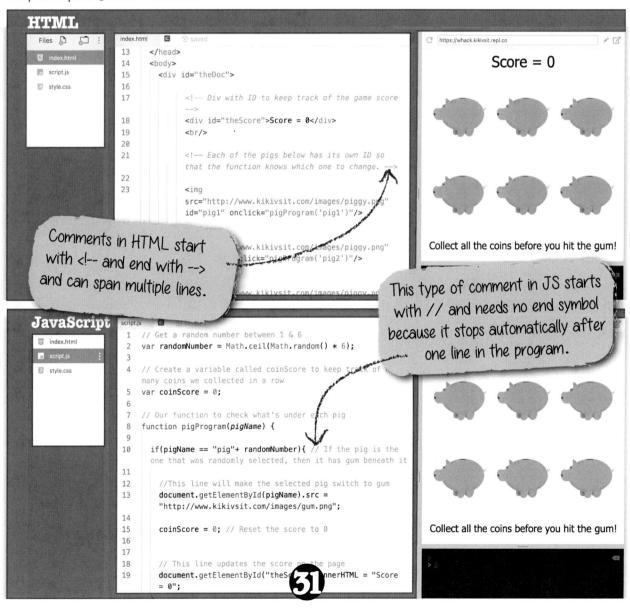

HTML

```
13    </head>
14    <body>
15        <div id="theDoc">
16
17            <!-- Div with ID to keep track of the game score
                 -->
18            <div id="theScore">Score = 0</div>
19            <br/>
20
21            <!-- Each of the pigs below has its own ID so
                 that the function knows which one to change. -->
22
23            <img
                 src="http://www.kikivsit.com/images/piggy.png"
                 id="pig1" onclick="pigProgram('pig1')"/>

                 www.kikivsit.com/images/piggy.png
                 lick="pigProgram('pig2')"/>

                 www.kikivsit.com/images/piggy.pn
```

Score = 0

Collect all the coins before you hit the gum!

Comments in HTML start with <!-- and end with --> and can span multiple lines.

This type of comment in JS starts with // and needs no end symbol because it stops automatically after one line in the program.

JavaScript

```
script.js
1    // Get a random number between 1 & 6
2    var randomNumber = Math.ceil(Math.random() * 6);
3
4    // Create a variable called coinScore to keep track of
     many coins we collected in a row
5    var coinScore = 0;
6
7    // Our function to check what's under each pig
8    function pigProgram(pigName) {
9
10       if(pigName == "pig"+ randomNumber){ // If the pig is the
         one that was randomly selected, then it has gum beneath it
11
12           //This line will make the selected pig switch to gum
13           document.getElementById(pigName).src =
             "http://www.kikivsit.com/images/gum.png";
14
15           coinScore = 0; // Reset the score to 0
16
17
18           // This line updates the score on the page
19           document.getElementById("theS      nnerHTML = "Score
             = 0";
```

Collect all the coins before you hit the gum!

Unlimited piggies
(Refreshing clicked pigs)

We've added another function that gets called when your mouse leaves the last place you clicked. It's supposed to replace the piggy but the program isn't working. Can you figure out why?

https://repl.it/@KIKIvsIT/resets

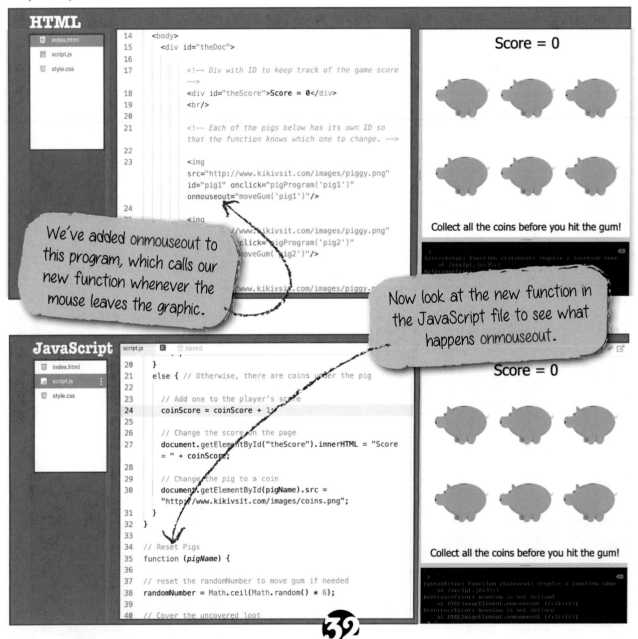

HTML

index.html
script.js
style.css

```
14   <body>
15     <div id="theDoc">
16
17       <!-- Div with ID to keep track of the game score
         -->
18       <div id="theScore">Score = 0</div>
19       <br/>
20
21       <!-- Each of the pigs below has its own ID so
         that the function knows which one to change. -->
22
23       <img
         src="http://www.kikivsit.com/images/piggy.png"
         id="pig1" onclick="pigProgram('pig1')"
         onmouseout="moveGum('pig1')"/>
24
25       <img
         src="http://www.kikivsit.com/images/piggy.png"
         id="pig2" onclick="pigProgram('pig2')"
         onmouseout="moveGum('pig2')"/>

         www.kikivsit.com/images/piggy.
```

> We've added onmouseout to this program, which calls our new function whenever the mouse leaves the graphic.

> Now look at the new function in the JavaScript file to see what happens onmouseout.

Score = 0

Collect all the coins before you hit the gum!

JavaScript   script.js   🖫   ⟳ saved

index.html
script.js
style.css

```
20     }
21     else { // Otherwise, there are coins under the pig
22
23       // Add one to the player's score
24       coinScore = coinScore + 1;
25
26       // Change the score on the page
27       document.getElementById("theScore").innerHTML = "Score
         = " + coinScore;
28
29       // Change the pig to a coin
30       document.getElementById(pigName).src =
         "http://www.kikivsit.com/images/coins.png";
31     }
32   }
33
34   // Reset Pigs
35   function (pigName) {
36
37     // reset the randomNumber to move gum if needed
38     randomNumber = Math.ceil(Math.random() * 6);
39
40     // Cover the uncovered loot
```

Score = 0

Collect all the coins before you hit the gum!

Now for something different

(Fill in the blanks)

Build a new
program with Kiki

This is completely different from the last program and there is a lot of JS code missing. Can you read the comments, then use what you've learned to finish this game?

https://repl.it/@KIKIvsIT/think

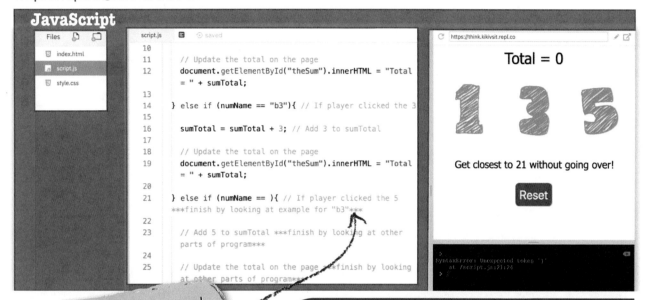

*There are 6 lines that need to be fixed. Look for the *** symbol for hints.*

You can do this!

Look at the other programs that you've made for examples of how to finish this one.

You'll need to...

- **Finish the else if for "b5"**

- **Add 5 to the variable sumTotal**

- **Reset sumTotal to zero**

- **Update the total on the page**

- **Create a page alert**

Mystic phrases
(Our final broken program)

Debug the program with Kiki

Here's another twist on the click-a-button formula. This time, when you click the crystal ball, you're supposed to get a mystic phrase. So, why doesn't it work?

https://repl.it/@KIKIvsIT/mystic

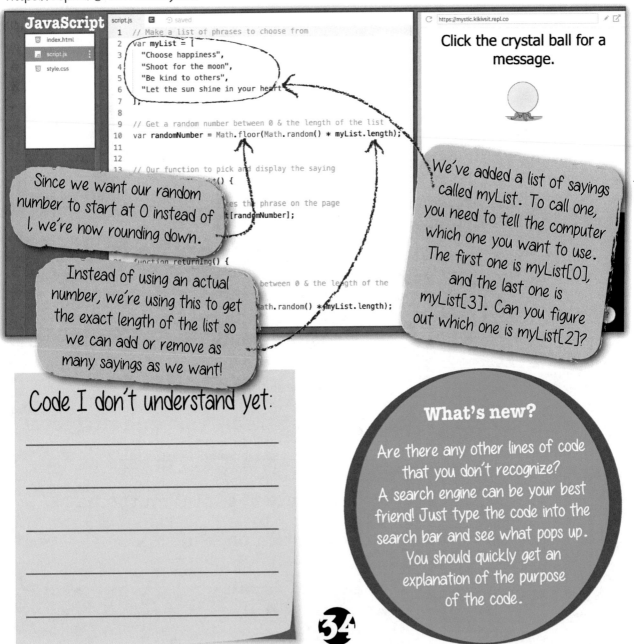

```
script.js                saved
1   // Make a list of phrases to choose from
2   var myList = [
3     "Choose happiness",
4     "Shoot for the moon",
5     "Be kind to others",
6     "Let the sun shine in your heart"
7   ];
8
9   // Get a random number between 0 & the length of the list
10  var randomNumber = Math.floor(Math.random() * myList.length);
11
12
13  // Our function to pick and display the saying
          ...() {
              ...es the phrase on the page
              t[randomNumber];

21  function returnImg() {
              ...between 0 & the length of the
              ath.random() * myList.length);
```

https://mystic.kikivsit.repl.co

Click the crystal ball for a message.

Since we want our random number to start at 0 instead of 1, we're now rounding down.

Instead of using an actual number, we're using this to get the exact length of the list so we can add or remove as many sayings as we want!

We've added a list of sayings called myList. To call one, you need to tell the computer which one you want to use. The first one is myList[0], and the last one is myList[3]. Can you figure out which one is myList[2]?

Code I don't understand yet:

_____

_____

_____

_____

_____

34

What's new?

Are there any other lines of code that you don't recognize? A search engine can be your best friend! Just type the code into the search bar and see what pops up. You should quickly get an explanation of the purpose of the code.

Use your imagination
(Make a program of your own)

Watch Kiki go through the process of starting a program

It can be a lot of fun to change someone else's code but it's really satisfying to make your own program from scratch! Take what you've learned here and mix it up into a program from your imagination. You can plan your program in advance or just start coding and see what happens. It's up to you!

I can do anything!

Don't limit yourself to the things that you have learned here. If you want to do something new and different, there are tutorials all over the internet that will show you how. Just do a quick online search and nothing will be out of reach.

There are so many ways to make this happen. Would you have add/subtract buttons to change your guess? A submit button to share your guess? Or would you have a text box to enter your guess? Can you use the internet to figure out how to add a text box to your page and to use the number inside later in your code?

Some ideas you can try:

- An answer to your questions
  Like the mystic phrases, but each phrase is just a form of "yes" or "no".

- Guess my number
  Have the computer "think" of a random number that you guess by pressing one of three buttons.

- Bird counter
  Look outside and check for birds. Click a button each time you see one and have the computer add to your variable. Can you add a reset?

- 50/50 chance
  Put two buttons on the screen. Have one be a winner and one be a loser randomly each time.

35

Answers

(Where's the bug?)

It doesn't work (Page 10) -

Line 2 of the myProgram() function is supposed to be
```
alert ("clicked");
```
but the parentheses are missing!

Variable soup (Page 16) -

Line 3 of the bugProgram() function tries to use the variable `BugName`, but the variable is supposed to be `bugName`, with a lowercase 'b'.

Who's got the button? (Page 22) -

Line 18 of the HTML file doesn't call any function! Instead of `<button onclick="()">` it should say `<button onclick="buttonProgram()">`.

Follow the ball (Page 26) -

Line 10 of the JS file doesn't give the right information. There is no element called "cup". Instead, the line should read:
```
document.getElementById("cup3").src =
```

Collect the coins (Page 30) -

Notice that the debugging console says that `pigName` is not defined. That's because the pigProgram() function isn't asking for a paramenter in the JS file. If you change line 5 of the JS file from
```
function pigProgram() {
```
to
```
function pigProgram(pigName) {
```
then you should be good to go!

Unlimited piggies (Page 32) -

The console gives you the biggest clue when it says "Function statements require a function name." That's because the name has been left off our second function in the JS file. Line 35 should read:

```
function moveGum(pigName) {
```

Something different (Page 33) -

This program is a hide-and-seek of missing code. Altogether, there are six lines of code that need to be either edited or added. You can figure out where these are by looking for the triple asterisks (***).

1) Line 21 should be: `} else if (numName == "b5"){`

2) Line 23 should be: `sumTotal = sumTotal + 5;`

3) Line 25 should be :
`document.getElementById("theSum").innerHTML = "Total = " + sumTotal;`

4) Line 29 should be: `sumTotal = 0;`

5) Line 31 should be:
`document.getElementById("theSum").innerHTML = "Total = " + sumTotal;`

6) Line 37 should be something like: `alert ("Sorry, you lose.");`

Mystic phrases (Page 34) -

This one is tough because the bug doesn't cause an error for the browser, only in the way the program runs. If you look carefully, though, you'll see that the line that's supposed to update the phrase on the screen is incomplete. Line 17 should be:
`document.getElementById("theThought").innerHTML = myList[randomNumber];`

Glossary
(Words and their meanings)

bugs
Problems in the code or in the running of the program

code
The instructions that tell the computer what to do

comment
Messages that a human can read but a computer can't

console
The screen that shows feedback from the computer

CSS (Cascading Style Sheets)
A file written in a special language to tell the computer how elements should look

debugging
Finding and fixing bugs

function
A named chunk of code that can be called from other places in the program

HTML (Hypertext Markup Language)
A language used to create webpages

input
Information that the user gives the computer

internet
The connected system of wires and computers that carry information across the world

JavaScript
A type of file that allows a webpage to change information without reloading

online
On the internet

parameter
A piece of information that you pass between elements of a program

program
A full set of code

programming
Writing programs

random
Picked without a noticeable pattern

royalty-free
Something you can use without having to pay a creator for each use

string
A group of characters that you want the computer to display in exactly the same way that you wrote it

tag
A piece of code that defines an element on a webpage

variable
A word or phrase that is used to symbolize a piece of information

webpage
A page on the internet

Index

(Where did we talk about it?)

Notes

(What are you thinking?)

Made in the USA
Middletown, DE
02 October 2020